Manchester
Then and Now

People, events and places from bygone years
and how the same locations look today

Manchester Evening News

iNostalgia

Text: ©2022 Malcolm Pheby, iNostalgia Ltd
Images: ©2022 Mirrorpix, Manchester Evening News
Design: Matt Rigby of moorsidemedia.co.uk
Malcolm Pheby has asserted his rights under Copyright, Designs and Patents Act 1988, to be identified as the author of this work.
The editors would like to acknowledge photographer Nicola Mazzuia for his contribution.
Published by iNostalgia, 355 Wilmslow Road, Fallowfield, Manchester. M14 6XU.
ISBN 978-1-84547-261-0

Then and Now – rediscovering Manchester's memorable past

There's no better way of gaining perspective on the wondrous kaleidoscope of life that is Manchester than by recapturing moments from the past and comparing them with the city as it is today.

Some places have changed little over the years, while others are unrecognisable. But every image and its modern counterpart tells a story – a story that helps give us all context and a sense of belonging at a time when we need it most.

The Covid pandemic and the grief it has brought have been felt deeply – in all areas of the community. Inevitably, some of the photos in this book reflect the restrictions and hardships we've faced.

Happy holidaymakers arriving back at Ringway Airport in the 1960s contrast sharply with the masks and protective clothing worn today.

But there are images of great inspiration too. They include the brilliant Duncan Edwards making his debut for Manchester United in 1953 and City bringing the FA Cup home in 1969.

We see schoolchildren saluting soldiers returning from the carnage of the First World War, suffragettes at Piccadilly Station and the spirit of hope in the Christmas crib at Strangeways prison.

Previous books have compared Manchester's past and present, but all the stories on these pages are new having been written especially for the popular Then and Now column in Manchester Evening News.

They've been described as a little slice of Manchester history.

We very much hope you enjoy them.

Malcolm Pheby

Opposite: Models Sue Dexter, left, and Jane Powell are pictured next to St Ann's Square sporting the latest trends for the Manchester Festival of May 1973. They were taking part in a Fashion Spectacular to highlight Manchester's textile heritage and hopes for the future.

Prince of Wales visits Manchester estate

In July 1933, the newly built housing estate in Broadoak Road, Wythenshawe, received a very important visitor – Britain's future king.

Our main image shows the dapper Prince of Wales, later King Edward VIII, touring homes with Mayor of Manchester Sir William Walker.

It was still a building site so the ground underfoot was a bit muddy – but the prince and the well-wishers who gathered to greet him don't seem to mind.

A spectator behind the policeman captured the moment on a Box Brownie camera.

Manchester, like most UK cities, was undergoing a housing boom in the 1930s. More than 4.3 million homes had been built since the 1920s.

Modern designs and building techniques, like those on display at Broadoak Road, helped fuel the housing expansion.

Low interest rates also increased home ownership. Only 10pc of families owned their own homes in 1914. The figure had risen to 31pc by 1939.

The Broadoak Road houses are still in place more than 80 years later as our current image testifies. Little has changed in the outlook, apart from the streetlamps and double-glazed windows!

King Edward VIII acceded to the English throne on January 20th 1936, but ruled for less than a year. He abdicated on December 11th to marry American divorcee Wallis Simpson.

During the Second World War, Edward was appointed Governor of the Bahamas.

After the conflict the couple lived in France and remained married until Edward's death in 1972.

Gorton marks Silver Jubilee in style

In May 1977, children celebrated the Queen's Silver Jubilee in Carberry Road, Gorton, with splendid shields and hats. The street is strewn with decorations and bunting.

The two-storey Victorian terraced houses are still in place in our modern snapshot – a reminder of the industrial expansion of Gorton when locomotive factories and other workshops sprang up in the area.

Chief among these was Beyer, Peacock and Company which built more than 8,000 locomotives for railways across the world from 1854 to 1966.

The Victorian Gothic masterpiece of Gorton monastery was a complete contrast to the hustle and bustle of the factories. Its frontage still soars above the red-brick terraced houses and shops today.

Completed in 1872, the monastery was designed by Edward Welby Pugin, the son of the famous Gothic revivalist Augustus Welby Pugin.

The church was Grade II listed in 1963, but closed for worship 20 years later in 1983.

In 1997, Gorton Monastery was placed on the Monuments Fund Watch List of the 100 most endangered sites in the world.

The church and friary buildings, however, were extensively restored in a £6 million project backed by the Heritage Lottery Fund, English Heritage and the European Regional Development Fund.

Gorton Monastery re-opened as a venue for conferences, meetings and community events in June 2007.

A memorial service for Gorton MP Sir Gerald Kaufmann was held at the monastery in March 2017.

Four years later, the monastery became the new home for the Manchester Camerata chamber orchestra.

When Deansgate was a haven for hikers!

Deansgate is deserted on the morning of Good Friday, April 1953, as two hikers set off to go pot-holing in the Manifold Valley, Derbyshire. There is no traffic apart from a solitary bus in the distance.

We even know the names of the intrepid hikers hidden behind their heavy loads. They are Brian Duckworth and George Evans of Monton, Lancashire. Hopefully they enjoyed a pleasant trip.

The scene is eerily similar to our modern image when Manchester's population was in lockdown due to the coronavirus. The usually bustling Deansgate is empty at a peak time of the day – a sight rarely witnessed in our lifetimes.

To the north, Deansgate runs to Victoria Street and Manchester Cathedral. At its southern end it connects with Chester Road and the Bridgewater Viaduct.

One of the most distinctive buildings on Deansgate is the neo-Gothic John Rylands Library. It was opened to the public in 1900 after being founded by Enriqueta Augustina Rylands in memory of her husband.

The northern part of Deansgate, linking to the Shambles, was badly damaged in the 1996 Manchester bombing. Its redevelopment included the No. 1 Deansgate building and the city branch of Harvey Nichols.

Other notable buildings on Deansgate are the Beetham Tower, the Royal Bank of Scotland and the remodelled Great Northern Warehouse.

Proud return of the Manchester Regiment

Soldiers march along London Road in 1919 after returning from Belgium at the end of the First World War.

The men are from the Manchester Regiment 8th Battalion. Crowds have gathered to welcome them home.

The regiment fought on the front line during the conflict, seeing action in the battles of the Marne, Aisne and Ypres.

Nine battalions were involved in the first day of the Battle of the Somme on July 1st 1916. They included the Manchester Pals – local men who enlisted together as part of Lord Kitchener's New Armies.

More than 57,000 men were killed, wounded or went missing that day – the deadliest in British Army history.

The war poet Wilfred Owen served with the Manchester Regiment, winning the Military Cross for his leadership at Joncourt. He was killed in action at the Sambre-Oise Canal one week before the Armistice was signed in November 1918.

The roots of the Manchester Regiment date back to 1685 when its forerunner, the Lancashire Militia, was raised by the Earl of Derby.

The regiment came into existence in its own right in 1881 when the Lancashire Militia amalgamated with the 63rd and 96th Regiment of Foot to form the Manchester Regiment.

In 1958, the Manchester Regiment was amalgamated with the King's Regiment (Liverpool) to form the King's Regiment (Manchester and Liverpool).

The roots of the Manchester Regiment date to 1685 when its forerunner, the Lancashire Militia, was raised by the Earl of Derby

In 2006, the regiment was amalgamated again – this time with the King's Own Royal Border Regiment and Queen's Lancashire Regiment – to form the current Duke of Lancaster's Regiment (King's, Lancashire and Border).

London Road is much quieter in our modern image. The busy street is almost empty as people stayed at home due to the coronavirus lockdown.

Stubby Kaye steps out in Quay Street

American film star Stubby Kaye arrives at Manchester Opera House in October 1966 to rehearse for the World Premiere of the show Man of Magic.

Also lining up outside the Quay Street theatre are co-stars Stuart Damon, centre, and Judith Bruce.

Kaye was best known for playing Nicely-Nicely Johnson in the 1950 film classic Guys and Dolls. He sang the show-stopping number Sit Down, You're Rockin' the Boat.

Damon went on to star as Craig Stirling in the TV series The Champions, while Bruce appeared in the TV series The Avengers and a number of films.

Quay Street is much quieter in our modern image as the coronavirus lockdown kept cars and pedestrians off the street.

The Opera House started life as the New Theatre in 1912 but was renamed the New Queen's Theatre in 1915. It became the Opera House in 1920.

It was a bingo hall for five years from 1979 to 1984 until it was bought by the Palace Trust.

Since then, the theatre has hosted major productions ranging from Phantom of the Opera and Ghost the Musical to the Gorillaz' ground-breaking show Demon Days Live.

Leonard Bernstein's musical West Side Story held its European premiere at the Opera House in 1958.

The Opera House and Palace Theatre on Oxford Street are now operated by the Ambassador Theatre Group.

Grand day out starts at the Shrewsbury Hotel

Pensioners outside the Shrewsbury Hotel in Clifton Street, Old Trafford, are eagerly looking forward to their coach trip to Blackpool.

The date is Wednesday 28th September 1966 and the weather appears dry, if a little overcast. Coats and cardigans are the order of the day.

A former Bass house, the Shrewsbury Hotel was a focal point for the community who lived round Clifton Street. It also used to be a regular meeting place for teams who competed on the playing fields behind the building.

By 2005, the hotel was in a derelict state. But it was restored at a cost of £450,000 to become part of the Afifah School in 2006. The school is still there today.

Terraced houses behind the hotel on Clifton Street have been replaced by residential blocks in our modern image, but the round-arched windows of the former hotel are instantly recognisable.

The urban area of Old Trafford grew massively after the building of the Manchester Ship Canal in the 1890s and the development of the Trafford Park Industrial Estate, providing jobs for thousands of workers.

More than 75,000 people were employed at Trafford Park at its peak in 1945, when the area had geared up to support the war effort. Rolls-Royce Merlin engines for the Spitfire and Lancaster bomber were manufactured there.

George Best – cricket star!

Manchester United winger George Best enjoys an impromptu game of cricket with youngsters outside his former digs on Aycliffe Avenue. The date is May 1968.

Best stayed at the Chorlton-cum-Hardy home of landlady Mrs Mary Fullaway shortly after he came to Manchester from Belfast in 1961 at the age of 15.

Dreadfully homesick, Best returned to Northern Ireland after only two days in England, but the club persuaded the gifted winger to come back to Manchester.

He had to play as an amateur for two years as English clubs were not allowed to sign Northern Irish players as apprentices at the time.

Best was given a job as an errand boy on the Manchester Ship Canal to allow him to train twice a week.

The future Northern Ireland international made his first team debut against West Bromwich Albion in September 1963 at the age of 17, but gained a regular place in the league-winning side the following season.

Best went on to make 361 league appearances for the Red Devils, scoring 137 goals, before leaving the club in 1974.

Best made 37 appearances for Northern Ireland from 1966 to 1977, scoring nine goals.

He won the European Ballon d'Or for being the continent's best player in 1968.

Chorlton grew as a Manchester suburb after the Midland Railway opened the local station in January 1880.

Further development took place after the First World War when the new council housing estate was built at Merseybank.

The houses are still standing today.

St Ann's Square – always fashionable

In 1900, St Ann's Square was already a chic place to shop - just as it is now.

High class boutiques nestled among imposing buildings in the city's most prestigious retail area.

Men looked resplendent in their top hats and walking canes while women wore long dresses and bonnets under a Victorian gas lamp.

Horse-drawn hansom cabs waited in line to take their elegant clients home over the old cobblestones.

The hustle and bustle of the turn of the 20th century is clearly evident, although the square is temporarily much quieter in our modern image due to social distancing and the strictures of the coronavirus lockdown.

Over recent years, Manchester has made its mark as the UK's second most popular location for retailers after London – confirming the success of areas like St Ann's Square, King Street and the ornate Barton Arcade.

The origins of St Ann's Square date back to 1227 when Henry II granted Robert Greslet, the Lord Mayor of Manchester, the right to hold a fair on St Matthew's Day.

St Ann's Church was consecrated in 1712 after an Act of Parliament decreed that a space 30 yards wide should be reserved for the fair.

The church still stands proudly in the square today.

The area was renamed St Ann's Square as a tribute to the reigning monarch, Queen Anne, and Lady Ann Bland, who was a local patron of the church.

When an outside broadcast was a rare event

A Granada TV crew interviews passers-by in Deansgate in March 1956.

A small crowd of onlookers has gathered round as outside broadcasts were few and far between. We believe this one was being filmed as part of a regional news programme for the Independent Television Authority (ITA) network.

Granada TV, founded by Sidney Bernstein at Granada Studios in Quay Street in 1954, did not begin transmissions in its own right until May 3rd 1956.

The opening night featured the programme Meet the People, hosted by American journalist and war correspondent Quentin Reynolds and entertainer Arthur Askey.

Unfortunately Reynolds had a little too much to drink before the broadcast and was forced to sober up!

ITV Granada is the only surviving company of the original four ITA franchises from 1954.

Its coverage area includes Greater Manchester and Merseyside. The Isle of Man was added from ITV Border in 2009.

Many new buildings have sprung up in this part of Deansgate since 1956 – as our modern image shows.

The Granada TV crew appear to be filming next to a bomb site from World War II which has now been paved over.

The street is quieter in our modern image than it was 60 years ago due to social distancing measures imposed by the coronavirus outbreak.

At the time of publication it was already returning to its usual hustle and bustle.

Remembering the cobblestones of Swan Street

Cars and trucks are trundling over the tram tracks and cobblestones of Swan Street, Ancoats, in January 1935.

A lone woman looks into the camera as litter blows around her feet. Across the road, men are going about their daily business.

The scene is much quieter in our modern image shot during coronavirus pandemic. There are no cars are on the street – and the area is almost deserted.

The cobblestones have been covered in tarmac and the trams have long since departed. Victorian buildings that were once warehouses and builders' yards have been converted to flats with shops below.

Smithfield Market is clearly visible in both images. Built in 1858, the market was roofed over with iron trusses in 1865.

By 1897, the market place occupied four and a half acres in the city centre. It stretched from Swan Street in Ancoats to Shudehill to the east and Oak Street to the west.

All kinds of food were available at Smithfield, which started life as a potato market. Fish, meat, fruit and vegetables were all on sale.

The market was also a centre for the Italian community who created an ice-cream manufacturing industry.

Smithfield Market closed in 1972 with stalls being relocated to the New Smithfield Market in Openshaw. The old market building was Grade II listed in 1973.

Stone and lino in Parker Street

Skilled stonemasons are busy at work in Parker Street, Manchester, in March 1932.

Behind them, at Numbers 2 to 4 Parker Street, is an imposing Victorian warehouse with the sign for Staines Inlaid Linoleums on the ground floor.

Lancashire was one of the centres for the linoleum industry along with East Scotland and the town of Staines itself. The Linoleum Manufacturing Company Ltd had offices at 2 Parker Street in 1927.

Linoleum was invented by Englishman Frederick Walton in 1855, when he noticed the durable qualities of solidified linseed oil (linoxyn) and thought it might make a cheap substitute for India rubber.

The highest grade linoleum in the 1930s was the inlaid type described in the sign. Joining and inlaying solid pieces of linoleum made it stronger and more durable.

Also occupying the warehouse behind the stonemasons was J.Templeton and Company – a Glasgow-based carpet manufacturer with offices in Manchester, London, Montreal and Melbourne.

The warehouses were destroyed in the Christmas Blitz of December 1940, when the Luftwaffe dropped nearly 500 tons of high explosive on Manchester over the course of two nights.

The scene is very different today. Concrete and glass office buildings have replaced the lino and carpet warehouses and tram tracks run through the street.

One person in a mask bears testament to the restrictions caused by the Covid 19 outbreak.

Mary Quant makes waves in Manchester

World-renowned fashion designer Mary Quant and her Ginger Group models are celebrating in Market Square in February 1966.

They'd just completed a photo shoot and were playing ring-o-roses round a lamp-post before taking part in a fashion show at Lewis's department store.

The only problem was that the models' hands got dirty and they had to dash back to the store to wash them before the next show!

Quant, centre, recognised Manchester's premier position in textiles when she launched her Ginger Group wholesale design and manufacturing company in 1963. The company offered up-to-date fashions at affordable prices.

An iconic figure of the '60s, Quant had a massive influence on female fashion. She made the mini-skirt popular and even gave it its name.

She also introduced another fashion craze – hot pants.

The look pioneered by Quant was quickly taken up by the stars of the time including Diana Rigg as Emma Peel in the popular TV programme The Avengers.

Men's fashion was led by Merseybeat and Manchester Beat groups including Herman's Hermits, the Hollies and, of course, the Beatles.

Their mop haircuts, collarless jackets and Cuban-heeled boots became all the rage.

Market Street looks a little quieter today. Traffic is banished and there a fewer pedestrians than normal as a result of coronavirus restrictions.

Trees, not present 50 years ago, provide greenery and shade on a summer afternoon.

Sombre wreath-laying in Southern Cemetery

A detachment of the National Fire Service solemnly salute the graves of colleagues who lost their lives in the Manchester Blitz of 1940.

The photograph, dating from December 1943, was taken in Southern Cemetery, Chorlton-cum-Hardy. The firemen carry a wreath to be laid in memory of their fallen comrades.

More than 680 people were killed in air raids on the nights of December 22nd and 23rd 1940, with 2,000 injured.

The Royal Exchange, Manchester Cathedral and the Free Trade Hall were among buildings badly damaged by Luftwaffe bombs.

The fire crews were in the thick of the action. More than 2,000 incendiary bombs were dropped on the city over two nights followed by 467 tons of high explosive.

The National Fire Service, created in August 1941, was an amalgamation of the wartime Auxiliary Fire Service and local authority fire brigades.

Its uniform was the dark blue double-breasted tunic of the AFS.

Southern Cemetery, opened in 1879, is the largest municipal cemetery in the UK and the second largest in Europe.

Many notable people are buried in the cemetery, including industrialist and philanthropist John Rylands and his wife Enriqueta, the founder of the John Rylands Library.

Manchester United manager Sir Matt Busby and Lady Jean Busby, as well as Manchester City player Billy Meredith, also lay in rest there.

Regimental Chapel rises again

Sunlight shines through the stained glass of the reconstructed Regimental Chapel at Manchester Cathedral in November 1951, shortly before its rededication in the presence of the Queen.

The chapel was destroyed on December 23rd 1940 when a German land-mine exploded just outside its north eastern corner. Not even the foundations survived.

The altar cross, candlesticks and memorial books had fortunately been removed to a safe place days before.

Rebuilding started in 1946 under architect Sir Hubert Worthington, who wanted to glaze all the windows in clear glass to bring light into the darkest part of the cathedral.

After Worthington's death in 1964, Margaret Traherne was commissioned to create a lasting memorial to him in the east window.

The clear glass was replaced with a vibrant mix of red and orange to symbolise fire and its associations with war, sacrifice and resurrection.

The window has become known as the 'Blitz Window' by old comrades of the Manchester Regiment as it reminded them of the flames that rose from the cathedral in 1940.

The colours can clearly be seen as light streams through the glass in our striking modern image, illuminating the regimental battle honours hanging from the walls.

The chapel was damaged again on Saturday June 15th 1996 when a 1,500 kilo lorry bomb was detonated by the Provisional Irish Republican Army (IRA) in Corporation Street.

Glass was blown out of the Worthington Memorial Window leading to further restoration work.

Art Deco in deepest Manchester

The striking Art Deco outline of the Kennet House council estate at Cheetham Hill dominates this archive image from November 1948

The contrast with today could not be more stark. Red-brick family homes have replaced the gleaming white oval structure once dubbed the Queen Mary due to its likeness to the ocean liner.

In the 1948 image, residents mill round the distinctive flats which dominate their elevated position as a solitary car climbs the hill.

Newly planted saplings are just starting to establish themselves; one may still be glimpsed as a mature tree in front of the homes in the 2019 photo.

Kennet House was built in 1934 to a design by Bolton-born architect Leonard Heywood. He was also responsible for new housing in Wythenshawe.

The flats heralded an era of high-rise developments where whole communities from terraced streets were transplanted into gleaming new multi-storey buildings.

Facilities at Kennet House included shops, a communal washroom, youth club and even a church. Each of the 181 flats had their own bathroom and hot and cold water.

But the promise of the 1930s had long
faded by the 1970s. Kennet House had
become run-down and poorly maintained.
It was eventually demolished in 1979.

Chethams' schoolboys salute wounded soldiers

Pupils at Chetham's School in Manchester welcome home the first wounded soldiers to return from France in late September 1914.

The First Battle of the Marne had just been fought, resulting in an Allied victory against the German armies in the west. It was the culmination of the German advance into France after invading Luxembourg and Belgium.

The mullioned stone frontage of Chetham's medieval stone buildings can clearly be seen behind the students. Modern, contemporary buildings are now also a feature of the site.

As far back as 1538, Chetham's Hospital and Library was described by the English poet and historian John Leland as a 'fair builded college'. It was about 100 years old when he put quill to paper.

Chetham's is probably the oldest continuously inhabited place in Manchester, possibly dating back to Saxon times.

The internationally renowned musical institution was originally a baronial manor house, converted to a college and later dissolved with the monasteries in Tudor times.

Thanks to the legacy of Manchester merchant Humphrey Chetham, the buildings were renovated in 1651. The college was refounded as a free public library and free school for 40 poor boys.

Specialising in music since the 1950s, the school now caters for almost 300 students, aged between eight and 18, selected by audition for their musical excellence.

Chetham's Library remains the oldest free public reference library in the English-speaking world.

Wartime centenary of Salford Cathedral

Horse carts still mingle with motor cars at Salford Cathedral in 1946 - a year after the end of the Second World War.

The Cathedral Church of St John the Evangelist, built between 1844 and 1848, is the seat of the Roman Catholic Bishop of Salford.

It was the first cruciform church to be built in England since the Reformation. The cathedral's spire, the tallest in Lancashire, was based on St Mary Magdalene's church in Newark-on-Trent.

St John's Church, as it was first known, became a cathedral in 1852 following the foundation of the Diocese of Salford in 1850. It was one of the first four Catholic cathedrals in England and Wales.

Built in the Neo-Gothic style, the cathedral was modelled on a number of medieval buildings.

The south front and nave resemble Howden Minster in Yorkshire while the choir echoes Selby Abbey, also in Yorkshire.

The total cost of building the cathedral was £18,000, of which £2,000 was donated by local businessmen Daniel Lee and John Leeming. Both are commemorated in chantries at the east end of the choir.

The spectacular stained glass east window depicts the Roman Catholic history of Christianity in England from St Augustine to the restoration of the Catholic hierarchy in 1850.

Our modern image shows a view of Salford Cathedral framed by the Sycamore Seed sculpture by Andrew McKeown in St Phillip's Square.

Lancaster bomber draws crowds at Piccadilly

In an era before social distancing, thousands of Mancunians crowd into Piccadilly for a close-up view of a Lancaster bomber.

The date is late August 1945 and Japan has just surrendered, signalling the end of World War II.

The reason for the gathering was a War Savings Campaign to support the war effort and immediate rebuilding for peacetime.

The locally built Avro Lancaster heavy bomber was a descendant of the twin-engined Avro Manchester developed in the 1930s.

Powered by four Rolls Royce Merlin engines, the Lancaster first saw service with Bomber Command in 1942. It quickly became the main aircraft for night-time raids.

Lancasters dropped 608,612 tons of bombs during the war, flying no less than 156,000 sorties. The Lancaster's long bomb bay enabled it to carry the RAF's largest explosives, including the 12,000lb Tall Boy and 22,000lb Grand Slam bombs.

Half the 7,000 Lancasters built were constructed at Avro's Woodford (Stockport) factory and at Chadderton (Oldham). Around 700 Lancasters were produced at the company's shadow factory at Leeds-Bradford Airport.

The Yorkshire factory was the largest building in Europe at the time, covering 1.5 million square feet. Its roof was heavily disguised by the addition of fields and hedges to confuse enemy planes.

Lancasters were most famously modified to carry the 'Bouncing Bomb' designed by Barnes Wallis to attack the Ruhr Valley dams in Operation Chastise in May 1943.

The raid breached the Edersee and Mohne dams, flooding the Eder and Ruhr valleys. Two hydro-electric power stations were also destroyed along with several factories and mines.

Airport departures – 1950s style!

It may look like a doctor's waiting room, but our image from February 1954 is actually the international departure gate at Manchester's Ringway Airport.

Instead of glitzy duty-free shops, cafes and restaurants, there are canvas chairs and a few pictures hung on the walls. Passengers were allowed to smoke before going through the doors to the airport apron and the waiting plane.

Ringway changed a lot during the 1950s. Buildings were refurbished, ground approach radar was installed and the runway was extended to allow larger aircraft to be handled.

In 1954, the year our photo was taken, British European Airways (BEA) launched an ambitious expansion programme to provide business travellers with an alternative means of getting to and from London.

The train took 3hrs 30mins to go from city centre to city centre. The plane could do the same journey in 1hr 25mins, plus the time it took to travel to or from the airport at either end.

The plane was more expensive at nearly £4 one way, while British Rail charged just over £2 for a first class ticket.

But the flights proved popular. By the end of 1956, BEA was carrying 60,000 passengers on the route.

In December 1954, Ringway reached the milestone of carrying its millionth passenger since reopening after the war in 1946.

Manchester Airport now has three passenger terminals and a cargo terminal. In 2019 it was the third busiest airport in the UK for passenger numbers – and the busiest outside London.

The bright new departure area at Manchester Airport looks very different today, albeit quieter due to Coronavirus restrictions.

Odeon in the dark – in the middle of the day!

Pedestrians look like they're picking their way through the fog on a cold evening on Oxford Street in November 1953.

The lights of Boots the chemist and the Odeon and Plaza cinemas twinkle in the gloom as cars drive with full headlights in the rain.

But, believe it or not, this photograph was not taken at night or even late afternoon. It was shot at 1.30pm – the middle of the day!

Smog – a mixture of smoke and fog – has descended on the city. It was commonplace in the 1950s and early 1960s as the atmosphere became thick with fumes from home fires and factories.

In some areas, the yellowy brown smog was so dense that it was impossible to see more than a few yards.

The air smelt of eggs due to the presence of sulphur dioxide.

Smog was caused by smoke being trapped by an anti-cyclone pushing rising air back down.

Research estimated that 4,000 to 12,000 people in the UK died as a result of smog in 1952 and a further 100,000 were taken ill.

One of Manchester's solutions to the pollution problem was to introduce fog pilots – a motorcycle combination fitted with powerful lamps front and back to guide buses through the smog.

The soot and grime on Manchester's buildings have all but disappeared today as a result of measures introduced after the Clean Air Act of 1956.

Suffragettes stand proud at the station

Manchester suffragette Emmeline Pankhurst, centre, is pictured outside Piccadilly Station in January 1913 in this historic archive image.

Pankhurst was 55 at the time and suffragette political activity was at its height. The women with her are believed to be Lady Constance Lytton, right, and possibly Sarah Jane Baines.

It was the same year Emily Davison died after falling under the King's horse at the Derby and the cactus house at Manchester's Alexandra Park was damaged by a suffragette bomb.

Fortunately no-one was hurt as the device went off at 4.20am. Local residents thought it was a gas explosion.

A merchant's daughter from Moss Side, Pankhurst was named as one of the most important people of the 20th century by Time magazine in 1999.

Her pioneering work as a suffragette in the early 1900s was crucial to women getting the vote in Britain.

After a lifetime of campaigning, Pankhurst died on June 14th 1928 - weeks before the Conservative government extended the vote to all women aged over 21 in the Representation of the People Act.

Piccadilly Station itself has changed hugely since 1913. The five-year refurbishment from the late 1990s to the early 2000s – evident in our modern image - cost £100 million and was the most expensive improvement on the UK rail network in its day.

Cantilever stand takes shape at Old Trafford

Here are two views, only two years apart, that capture a Manchester sporting landmark during construction and later in its full completed glory.

The landmark in question is Old Trafford football ground and our main image from March 1965 shows the first cantilever stand taking shape.

The familiar faces training beneath it are Manchester United players Denis Law, goalkeeper Pat Dunne, Paddy Crerand, George Best and Tony Dunne.

It was the approach of the 1966 FIFA World Cup that prompted United directors to redesign the United Road (north) stand to remove the pillars obstructing the view of spectators.

The stand was also extended to hold 20,000 spectators, 10,000 of whom would be seated.

Old Trafford was due to host Portugal's matches in Group 3, so it needed to look its best. As it happened, Portugal and the tournament's top scorer Eusebio beat Hungary and Bulgaria in Manchester and then defeated Brazil 3-1 at Goodison Park.

Our second image, from August 1967, shows the new cantilever stand nearly full at the start of a new season. And what a season it turned out to be!

The Red Devils became the first English club to win the European Cup when they beat Benfica 4-1 in extra time at Wembley.

It was also the season George Best came into his own. The Northern Ireland winger was the club's top scorer with 32 goals in all competitions, as well as being named European Footballer of the Year.

United nearly won the league too. They were pipped at the post by Manchester City after losing the last game of the season to Sunderland.

Wartime bombs devastate cathedral

Wartime bombs severely damaged Manchester Cathedral during the Luftwaffe raids of December 1940.

The medieval Lady Chapel was destroyed along with the cathedral roofs and the Stanley chantry chapel. All the stained glass windows were blown out.

Ancient stonework and charred timbers are piled high in our picture as stunned civilians walk round the wreckage. It was little wonder that repairs took almost two decades to complete.

The cathedral was not the only building damaged in what became known as the Christmas Blitz of December 1940. The Royal Exchange and Free Trade Hall were also badly hit.

Heavy raids on the nights of December 23 and 24 saw more than 2,000 incendiary bombs dropped on the city along with 467 tons of high explosive.

An estimated 684 people were killed and another 2,000 injured in the raids, which mainly targeted the industrial complex of Trafford Park.

Much of the current cathedral dates to 1421, when it was built as the parish church of St Mary, St George, the patron saint of England and St Denys, the patron saint of France.

The church maintained a college of priests who were housed in new buildings that survive today as Chetham's Library. The parish church became a cathedral in 1847.

Our modern image shows the cathedral gardens in more tranquil times with leaves falling in November.

Keith Richards mobbed in Manchester

Rolling Stones' guitarist Keith Richards does his best to leave Manchester as eager fans press him for his autograph in St Peter's Square.

The date is March 1965 and the group had probably just finished filming the TV show Scene at Six-Thirty at Granada studios.

The half-hour daily news, entertainment and current affairs programme ran from 1963 to 1966 and often featured the biggest bands of the day.

Presenters included Brian Truman, Bill Grundy, Chris Kelly and Michael Parkinson. The show often featured groups in the studio before their singles hit the charts – stealing a march on their London-based opposition.

The Stones were certainly riding high in March 1965. They'd notched up three UK Number One singles with It's All Over Now and Little Red Rooster in 1964, and The Last Time in February 1965.

As well as Richards, the 1965 Rolling Stones' line-up featured Mick Jagger on lead vocals, Brian Jones on guitar, Bill Wyman on bass and Charlie Watts on drums.

The group went on to become one of the best-selling bands of all time with record sales in excess of 200 million.

Billboard magazine ranked them second in their list of the world's greatest artists in 2019.

The Stones have also won three Grammy Awards and were inducted into the Rock and Roll Hall of Fame in 1989.

Behind Richards in our main image is the Manchester Cenotaph - still in its original position. Designed by Sir Edwin Lutyens, it was inaugurated in 1924.

The monument was relocated to its current site at the north-east end of St Peter's Square in 2014 to make way for the expanded Metrolink network.

Also visible is the memorial cross by the architect Temple Moore. It marks the former location of St Peter's Church, demolished in 1907.

Christmas tree lights up Victoria Station

The true spirit of the festive season is captured as staff switch on the splendid Christmas tree at Manchester Victoria station in December 1951.

Spectators at the event said the tree brightened up the whole building in the austere years after World War II. The station itself was bombed during the Christmas Blitz of December 1940.

Performing the ceremony, in front of the station noticeboard, was District Passengers Superintendent Mr R.C. Flowerdew. He's standing proudly to the right of the picture.

Construction work on Manchester Victoria started in 1842. The official opening came on New Year's Day 1842 when the Manchester and Leeds Railway built an extension line from Miles Platting to the Hunts Bank site.

The station's name celebrated the monarch of the day. Manchester Victoria was expanded to 17 platforms in 1904 and the current main façade, designed by William Dawes, was built in 1909.

The parcels office and the roof over four platforms were damaged by Luftwaffe bombs in World War II. The office was rebuilt, but the platforms were left open.

Our modern image, from September 2016, reflects another happy occasion for the station. It shows the Flying Scotsman passing through – much to the delight of waiting steam enthusiasts.

Built in 1923 for the London to Edinburgh east coast route, the Flying Scotsman became the first steam locomotive to reach 100 miles per hour in November 1934.

It also achieved the longest non-stop run for a steam locomotive when it ran for 422 miles in Australia in August 1989.

Panto time on Coronation Street – oh yes it is!

The cast of Coronation Street staged their own version of the pantomime Cinderella at Granada studios in December 1964.

Local children from Manchester's Wood Street Mission were invited along to the rehearsals to see some of the nation's favourite soap characters in unfamiliar guise.

Pat Phoenix, Elsie Tanner in Coronation Street, was Prince Charming while Jennifer Moss (Lucille Hewitt) was Cinderella. Dennis Tanner (Philip Lowrie) took the role of Buttons and Gordon Rollings (Charlie Moffitt) played one of the Ugly Sisters.

They certainly look the part on stage in front of the cameras in Coronation Street's mission hall set.

All the children were treated to tea with the actors after the pantomime, which was aired on Wednesday December 23rd. The show ended on a rousing note with everyone singing the Beatles' song She Loves You.

By 1964, Coronation Street was recording its highest ever viewing figures with an average audience of 18.4 million. Launched on December 9th 1960, the Manchester-produced programme had quickly become the nation's favourite TV drama.

Moving forward to 2016, the pantomime at Manchester Opera House was Aladdin starring Ben Adams, Sherrie Hewson and John Thomson.

There was a strong Coronation Street connection as Hewson played Maureen Webster on the soap and Salford actor Thomson was children's entertainer Jesse Chadwick from 2008 to 2010.

Prisoners pay homage at Strangeways crib

Seasonal decorations and a Christmas crib adorn the normally austere interior of Strangeways Prison, Manchester, in December 1969.

Normally a Christmas tree would stand in the central hall, but prison staff and inmates opted for a crib instead. The customary tree was pushed up to the second floor balcony.

As well as putting up decorations, our photo shows prisoners rehearsing for the annual carol service due to be held around the crib.

Strangeways Prison, now HM Prison Manchester, was designed in the Victorian Gothic style by architect Alfred Waterhouse and opened in June 1868. It replaced the New Bailey Prison in Salford.

A prominent feature is the 234ft high ventilation tower which has become a local landmark. The walls of the prison are said to be 16ft thick.

The prison was rebuilt after the riots of April 1990 which saw 147 staff and 47 inmates injured, one fatally. A prison officer also died from heart failure.

The repair and modernisation programme cost more than £80 million, with rebuilding being completed in 1994.

Strangeways housed male and female prisoners up to 1963 when it became male only. Notable female prisoners included the suffragettes Christabel Pankhurst and Catherine and Helen Tolson.

Another suffragette, Emily Davison, was sentenced to a month's hard labour in 1909 for throwing rocks at the carriage of Chancellor of the Exchequer David Lloyd George.

Our modern image shows the exterior of the prison in 2014.

Braziers thaw out Maine Road pitch

Ground staff are desperately trying to thaw out the frozen pitch at Maine Road, Manchester, using braziers filled with hot coals. The date is January 8th 1953.

Work started in the morning and carried on well into the night. Straw was laid after the ice had melted to prevent the ground re-freezing.

The action was necessary to save the forthcoming FA Cup match between Manchester City and Swindon Town, scheduled to go ahead on Saturday January 10th.

All the hard work paid off as the game went ahead with the Blues romping home 7-0 against their Third Division opponents.

Four of City's goals came from inside forward Johnny Hart, who was in inspired form – despite the muddy pitch. The other scorers were Johnny Williamson, Bob Cunliffe and Ivor Broadis.

Unfortunately, City did not progress further in the competition as they were knocked out by Luton Town in the next round after a replay.

The first match at Maine Road ended in a 1-1 draw, but Luton won the replay 5-1.

Our second photo shows the Blues again in action on a slushy Maine Road surface, this time against Leicester City in the First Division in January 1995. The visitors won 1-0.

Maine Road was the Blues' Moss Side home from 1923 to 2003. City then moved to the City of Manchester Stadium in Ardwick, the place where the club originally formed in 1880.

City won the Premier League at their new home in 2018, becoming the only Premier League team to amass 100 points in a single season.

A year later, the Blues won the domestic treble of the league, FA Cup and League Cup as well as the Charity Shield. Top scorer for the season was Sergio Aguero with 32 goals in all competitions.

When Prince Charles dropped into the Rovers

A rowdy crowd seem to be drinking at the bar of the Rovers Return, Coronation Street, in April 1968, as cameras film the long-running soap opera.

Barmaid Emily Nugent, left, played by Eileen Derbyshire, and Hilda Ogden portrayed by Jean Alexander, are decidedly not amused.

Also taking a drink on the Coronation Street set is regular character Jerry Booth, second left, played by Graham Haberfield.

A focal point for many storylines over the years, the programme's pub was named after the well-known Rovers Return Inn that used to occupy a 14th century building in Withy Grove. It lost its licence in 1924 and was eventually pulled down in 1958.

The Coronation Street version of the Rovers, including the exterior, was originally set entirely inside Granada studios. All the houses were three-quarters scale which meant actors had to walk slowly past them to avoid looking abnormally large!

Production techniques at the time made it difficult to record and edit sequences filmed in different locations.

It was only in 1967 that the Street used separate interior and exterior sets.

The Rovers was transformed again in 1982 when the Queen opened an almost full-size set on the Granada backlot. It expanded again when filming moved from Quay Street studios to MediaCity to meet the demands of high-definition TV.

In 2000, Prince Charles popped into the Rovers for a whisky during the soap's 40th anniversary celebrations. Our photo shows him chatting to landlady Natalie Barnes, played by Denise Welch.

City bring the FA Cup home

The victorious Manchester City team proudly parade the FA Cup on an open-top bus outside the Town Hall. The date is April 27th 1969.

The Blues won the coveted trophy by beating Leicester City 1-0 at Wembley thanks to a goal from Fallowfield-born inside forward Neil Young.

Leading the celebrations on the left side of the bus is assistant manager Malcolm Allison along with midfielder Colin Bell, holding the cup aloft.

At the other end of the top deck are Mike Summerbee and Francis Lee along with a photographer precariously leaning over the side of the bus to get a better shot.

The FA Cup win capped a difficult season for reigning First Division champions City.

Manager Joe Mercer was hoping for another league title when the Blues thrashed West Bromwich Albion 6-0 in the opening match of the season – the Charity Shield.

But it was not to be. City finished in 11th place on 41 points, well adrift of champions Leeds United on 67 points.

The Blues added two more trophies in the subsequent 1969-70 season when they won the European Cup Winners' Cup by defeating Gornik Zabrze 2-1 in Vienna and the League Cup by beating West Brom 2-1 at Wembley.

The upward angle of our original image sees the splendid Victorian Gothic Town Hall towering over the players. Designed by architect Alfred Waterhouse, the landmark building was completed in 1877.

The Town Hall was opened on September 13th 1877 by the Mayor, Abel Heywood, when Queen Victoria refused to attend. More than 14 million bricks were used in its construction.

Ingenious structural devices were installed to bring natural window light into the Victorian Gothic-style building. These included suspended first floor rooms, made possible by an iron-framed construction, dormer windows and skylights

George V greets players at Hyde Road

King George V visits Manchester City's Hyde Road stadium to watch the Blues play Liverpool in the First Division. The date is March 27th 1920.

It was the first time a reigning monarch had attended a match at a football venue outside London.

The linesmen and referees look smart in their blazers while the king is wearing spats over his shoes for the occasion. He's also carrying an umbrella for good measure!

City won the match 2-1 with both goals coming from Horace Barnes. It made up for the 1-0 league defeat City suffered at Anfield a week earlier.

The Blues went on to finish seventh in the league with 45 points, two points behind Bolton Wanderers. Barnes was City's top scorer for the season with 23 goals in all competitions.

The Hyde Road stadium in West Gorton was home to the Blues from 1887 to 1923.

The club were looking for a new stadium from November 1920 when a fire destroyed the main stand.

Over the years, Maine Road hosted England internationals, FA Cup semi-finals and even a League Cup Final. Its nickname was the Wembley of the North.

It still holds the record for the highest attendance for a club in their normal stadium – 84,569 for the 1934 FA Cup Sixth Round match against Stoke City. The Blues won 4-2.

Hyde Road stadium was demolished once the move to the 80,000 capacity Maine Road ground in Moss Side had been completed in 1923. A section of the roofing is still in use on a stand at The Shay stadium, Halifax.

The Blues left Maine Road in 2003 for the City of Manchester Stadium situated near Ardwick where the club first formed in 1880.

Radiant future Queen inspects her troops

Princess Elizabeth, our future Queen, reviews troops in Albert Square. It is March 1949, just four years after the end of the Second World War.

Accompanying the Princess on her tour of inspection is her husband the Duke of Edinburgh and Colonel R.D. Martin Bird.

In February 1945, Princess Elizabeth was appointed as an honorary second subaltern in the Auxiliary Territorial Service – the women's branch of the army. Her service number was 230873.

She was later promoted to the rank of junior commander (the female equivalent of a captain) after training as a driver and mechanic.

Prince Philip joined the Royal Navy at the age of 18 in 1939 and served with distinction in the Mediterranean and Pacific fleets during the war.

The Royal couple were married at Westminster Abbey on November 20th 1947. As rationing was still in force, Princess Elizabeth needed to use coupons to buy material for her dress.

Prince Charles was born in November 1948, three months before the Manchester visit. The couple's second child, Princess Anne, was born in August 1950.

Albert Square has strong connections with royalty. Our second image shows its focal point, the Albert memorial, which was unveiled in 1867.

It was built in memory of Queen Victoria's Consort Prince Albert who died in 1861. The cost was met by public donations.

The surrounding land was undeveloped at the time the memorial was constructed. The imposing Town Hall was not built until 1877.

Hungarian legend Puskas lands at Ringway

Four of the greatest footballers of all time have gathered at Ringway Airport, Manchester, in March 1965.

Three of them had flown into Manchester for the testimonial match of English soccer legend Sir Stanley Matthews, second left, due to take place in Stoke the following day.

Matthews is clearly overjoyed to welcome Spain and Real Madrid forward Alfredo di Stefano, left, and Hungarian superstars Ferenc Puskas and Laszlo 'Laddie' Kubala.

Di Stefano was described as the 'most complete footballer in the history of the game.' He played mainly as a forward, earning the nickname 'Saeta Rubia' or 'the Blond Arrow'.

His skill, stamina and versatility helped Real Madrid dominate the European Cup and La Liga throughout the 1950s.

Prolific scorer Puskas was part of the Hungarian 'Golden Team' that beat England twice in 1953, first with a shock 6-3 win at Wembley and then 7-1 in Budapest. Puskas scored twice in each game.

Kubala, also an attacker, was renowned for powerful finishing and pinpoint accuracy from fee kicks. He was a key member of the Barcelona team of the 1950s, scoring 280 goals in 345 appearances.

By the mid-1960s, Ringway Airport had launched the first transatlantic flight originating in Manchester. In 1969, the runway was extended to 2,745 metres enabling aircraft to fly non-stop to Canada.

In contrast to the warmth of the 1965 welcome, recent travellers to Manchester Airport faced all the restrictions of the Covid lockdown as our modern photo clearly demonstrates.

City players on their way to Wembley!

Manchester City footballers carry their match-day suits ready to board the London train at Piccadilly Station at the end of April 1969.

They were on their way to the capital for a very important date – the FA Cup Final against Leicester City at Wembley.

Pictured, from left, are Alan Oakes, Mike Doyle, Colin Bell, Neil Young and Tony Coleman.

Little did he know it, but Young was to play a pivotal role in the match against the East Midlands' side. He scored the only goal in City's 1-0 victory – a left-footed shot from Mike Summerbee's cross in the 24th minute.

The match was memorable for two extremes. At 21, Leicester full back David Nish was the youngest ever captain of a cup final team. In contrast, City skipper Tony Book became the third oldest at 35.

The Blues brought the cup back to Manchester the evening after the final. They travelled by train to Wilmslow where they switched to an open-topped bus to the Town Hall.

More than 25,000 fans lined the route while another 3,000 packed Albert Square to greet their heroes. City paraded the cup at Maine Road three days later at their First Division match against West Ham.

The scene at Manchester Piccadilly Station was very different in early 2021. Masks and social distancing held sway as the city was locked down due to Corona virus restrictions.

Best wins the coveted Ballon d'Or

Manchester United winger George Best is delighted to receive the prestigious Ballon d'Or trophy for being European Footballer of the Year.

The date is April 1969, just before the league match against Burnley which the Red Devils won 2-0. Best was on the scoresheet along with an own goal from Colin Waldron.

Sharing the spotlight with Best are fellow players and previous Ballon d'Or winners Bobby Charlton, suited, and Denis Law. Charlton was awarded the coveted trophy in 1966, England's World Cup-winning year, and Law in 1964.

Watching the proceedings with pride is outgoing United manager Sir Matt Busby. He was stepping down at the end of the season after 24 years at the helm to be replaced by Wilf McGuinness.

Fast forward 31 years to August 2000 and Best, Charlton and Law are back on the Old Trafford pitch once again to receive Lifetime Achievement Awards from the club.

The presentation took place at half time during the Premier League match between the Red Devils and Newcastle United. The result was again a 2-0 win for United with goals from Andrew Cole and Ronny Johnsen.

Known as the United Trinity, Best, Charlton and Law are commemorated by a statue unveiled outside Old Trafford in 2008.

Team-mate Paddy Crerand summed them up by saying: 'However tough the match was, you always knew Bobby could unleash one of his strikes from God-knows-where, Denis would make something out of nothing inside the box or George would just do something magical'.

It was a fitting tribute to the brilliant talents of three outstanding players for United – each a football legend in their own right.

All wrapped up at Longsight Cricket Club

It doesn't appear too warm as spectators watch the action at Longsight Cricket Club in July 1953. Coats and hats are clearly the order of the day!

Factory chimneys and terraced houses can be glimpsed in the distance as a reminder of the area's industrial heritage. Both have disappeared in our modern image.

There's a new pavilion too and benches now face a bowling green rather than a cricket pitch.

Redbrick terraces are still a feature of Longsight. Other buildings include Edgar Wood's Grade I listed First Church of Christ Scientist and the former homes of Emmeline Pankhurst and Charles Halle.

The Pankhursts' family home was situated on the fringes of Longsight at Plymouth Grove.

Longsight grew massively in the Victorian era and early 20th century. In the 1840s, the area was described as just a few buildings in a rural setting.

Much of Longsight was demolished and rebuilt as terraces were cleared in the 1960s as part of a major redevelopment scheme.

Longsight railway station closed in 1958, but the West Coast Main Line from Manchester to Stockport still passes through the area.

Longsight Cricket club was founded in 1848 and played two matches against the Australian touring team in 1878. The Aussies were captained by D.W. Gregory and Longsight's guest player was none other than the legendary W.G. Grace.

Longsight won one of the matches by two wickets and drew the other.

The cricket club was closed for business in 2004 and the site redeveloped for housing a decade later. A new clubhouse was built next to the bowling green.

Downcast Eusebio leaves the 1966 World Cup

Portuguese soccer legend Eusebio sits alone at Manchester Piccadilly Station in July 1966 after his country's exit from the World Cup.

Portugal were knocked out at the semi-final stage by eventual winners England. The score was 2-1.

Eusebio was brilliantly marked by tenacious Manchester United midfielder Nobby Stiles while club team-mate Bobby Charlton scored both of England's goals.

Eusebio had become a familiar figure in Manchester as Portugal played all their group matches in the North West, including two at Old Trafford.

They beat Hungary 3-1 in front of a crowd of 31,000 and Bulgaria 3-0.

There was a slight diversion at the Hungary match when Portuguese player Morays rescued an injured thrush that had fluttered on to the pitch!

Portugal also defeated Brazil 3-1 at Goodison Park in the group stage with Eusebio netting twice.

They then overcame North Korea 5-3 in the quarter final. This time Eusebio scored four!

The Portuguese forward at least had the consolation of ending the tournament as the top scorer with nine goals.

Eusebio appears to be taking little comfort from the achievement back at the station – with autograph hunters waiting at a respectful distance.

Surrounded by kit bags and, of course, an umbrella in case of Manchester rain, Eusebio looks lost in thought.

There are no fans – and hardly any commuters - in our modern photo of Manchester Piccadilly in the Covid lockdown.

Cinema with a long, long drinks bar!

The final days of the well-known Gaumont Cinema in Oxford Street, a popular venue for moviegoers from its opening in 1935, are captured in our main image from January 1974.

The 2,300 seater cinema was built in the Italian Renaissance style by the Granada Group on the site of the former Hippodrome Theatre.

It included one of the longest licensed bars in the North – so there was ample space to serve thirsty customers on busy nights!

The first film shown at the Gaumont on its opening night on October 21st 1935 was Alfred Hitchcock's The 39 Steps, starring Manchester-born actor Robert Donat and Madeleine Carroll.

The opening ceremony was conducted by movie stars Jessie Matthews and Sonnie Hale, with Stanley Tudor playing the Wurlitzer organ.

In the 1950s and 60s, the Gaumont hosted long runs of popular films. These included the Rodgers and Hammerstein musicals South Pacific, which ran there for two years from 1958, and the Sound of Music from 1965 to 1967.

One of the final films shown was Carry On Abroad starring Joan Sims, Charles Hawtrey, Sid James and Stockport actor Peter Butterworth.

After its closure in January 1974, the ground floor and basement of the Gaumont became Rotters Nightclub. The building was demolished after Rotters shut down in 1990.

Standing in its place, as can be seen from our modern image, is a multi-storey car park. The neighbouring three-storey Victorian building remains intact and is now partially occupied by a fast-food restaurant.

Duncan Edwards makes his debut

Saturday April 4th 1953 marked a historic moment for Manchester United – the debut of football icon Duncan Edwards.

The brilliant all-rounder is pictured leaving the Old Trafford pitch after a 4-1 defeat by Cardiff City. United's only goal was scored by Roger Byrne.

It was a time of transition for United who finished eighth in the First Division with 46 points. Manager Matt Busby was bringing in a group of highly talented young players who would later become famous as the Busby Babes.

As well as Edwards, forward Dennis Viollet and defender Jackie Blanchflower would join the team. The 1952-3 season also saw the arrival of 21-year-old centre-forward Tommy Taylor from Barnsley for a club record transfer fee of £29,999.

But Edwards was the true baby of the side. He was just 16 years and 185 days old when he made his debut, making him the youngest player ever in the top flight in English football.

Edwards came into the United team at a time when manager Matt Busby was bringing a number of youngsters through the ranks to bolster some aging professionals.

The newcomers included Dennis Viollet and Jackie Blanchflower and became known as the Busby Babes.

The talented youngsters were a tight-knit bunch. They stayed together at Mrs. Watson's homely Old Trafford guest house, eating their meals in a jacket and tie!

After a short but glittering career, which many predicted would see him become England captain, Edwards died as a result of injuries sustained in the Munich air crash of February 1958. He was 21.

A heartfelt tribute to Edwards came from fellow United legend and team-mate Bobby Charlton, also pictured on the Old Trafford pitch in April 2016.

He said of Edwards: 'Physically he was enormous. He was strong and had a fantastic football brain. His ability was complete.'

Granada TV takes to the air

Final checks are being made at Granada studios the night before going on air for the very first time on Wednesday May 2nd 1956.

Looking toward the ceiling among the cameras and cables at Quay Street is Granada's founder Sidney Bernstein.

Keen to save money, he built the studios on a modular basis. Units were left unfinished until there was a demand for them.

Granada bought the Quay Street site from Manchester City Council for £82,000. Part of the Manchester and Salford Junction Canal ran in a tunnel beneath it.

The opening night proved eventful as journalist and presenter Quentin Reynolds turned up inebriated before interviewing Arthur Askey on the programme Meet the People – and had to be sobered up!

Although the studios were designed by architect Ralph Tubbs, Bernstein's influence was keenly felt. Granada producer Jeremy Isaacs described him as a 'genial tyrant', overseeing almost every aspect of the work.

The studios went on to produce many famous programmes including Coronation Street from 1960 onwards, Brideshead Revisited, World in Action and the Krypton Factor.

Bernstein was it enthusiastic about Coronation Street at the start. Neither was his brother Cecil. He felt that its creator Tony Warren had picked up all the 'boring bits' from his original proposal Florizel Street and strung them all together!

In spite of the misgivings, Coronation Street got the go-ahead and quickly became a national favourite.

Granada also won acclaim for its current affairs and documentary programmes including World in Action, What the Papers Say and Disappearing World.

After the studios closed in November 2013, ITV Granada and ITV Studios moved to MediaCityUK in the Salford Quays where Coronation Street is currently filmed.

The soap was given a £10m new set with wider streets to allow cars to pass side by side.

Happy landings for Manchester holidaymakers

Here's how foreign travel looked at the arrivals gate at Manchester's Ringway Airport in June 1967.

This was the entry to Manchester for passengers flying in from around the world in the 1960s. Waiting family and friends could be glimpsed as the arrivals' door opened and closed.

Baggage could then be reclaimed as the sign above the gate explains – in English, French and German.

Air France started the ball rolling at Ringway with continental flights from Manchester in 1946 - and is still the airport's longest continuous operator. BOAC launched the first transatlantic flight to originate at Manchester in 1963.

The 1960s saw the growth of package holidays in Europe, particularly Spain.

Flying was still regarded as an adventure where people dressed in smart clothes and looked forward to luxury cabin service. Passengers could even smoke on planes.

By 1971, Manchester was handling more than two million passengers a year. A year later, the link road connecting the airport to the M56 was opened. The former RAF base was officially renamed Manchester International Airport in 1975.

There is little glamour or excitement in our modern image of arrivals taken in 2021. Covid protection regulations are in full swing.

Passengers flying from Abu Dhabi look like more like they've stepped out of a laboratory than a plane!

Facing up to the press at Old Trafford

The European Cup is being paraded for the press at Old Trafford after Manchester United became the first English club to win the coveted trophy. The date is July 25th 1968.

Two months earlier, United beat Portuguese club Benfica 4-1 in a thrilling final at Wembley that went to extra time.

After a goalless first half, Bobby Charlton scored in the 53rd minute only for Jaime Graca to equalise 11 minutes before full time. The Red Devils then scored three goals in seven minutes in extra time.

Best netted after a solo run, followed by a header from Brian Kidd – currently assistant coach at City – and then came a second goal for Charlton.

Back at Old Trafford, the press are getting extreme close-ups of the United players! Denis Law, who missed the final, is turning to talk to his team-mates while Best looks unperturbed.

He had every reason to be. The coveted Ballon d'Or award for European player of the year was coming his way – and he was so well-known that he'd earned the title El Beatle!

The name was given to him after a stunning performance against Benfica in Lisbon's Stadium of Light in March 1966. United won 5-1 with the 19-year-old Best scoring twice in the opening minutes.

Our modern image from April 2003 shows more press on the pitch at Old Trafford, this time to capture United's celebrations after winning the Premier League with a 3-0 victory over Aston Villa.

The season's top scorer, Robin van Persie, holds his arms aloft alongside Michael Carrick, Wayne Rooney and Rio Ferdinand.

Aussie cricketers stride out for the Ashes

Australian batsmen Warren Bardsley and Bill Woodfull walk purposefully to the crease on the final day of the Fourth Ashes Test at Old Trafford.

The date is July 27th 1926 and a bumper crowd is looking forward to witnessing some first class cricket after rain had disrupted much of the previous play.

The batsmen wore little in the way of protective headgear in the 1920s – just the famous Aussie green caps to face the England bowlers.

Undeterred, Woodfull scored a majestic 117 as Australia built up a total of 335 in 150.2 overs. In reply, England scored 305 for five wickets. The three-day match was drawn.

England eventually took the series 1-0 by winning the final Test at the Oval, London, by 289 runs.

Our second image from August 2005 shows Australian bowlers Brett Lee and Glen McGrath at the crease after earning their team a draw in the Ashes Third Test at Old Trafford.

England captain Michael Vaughan is about to shake the batsmen's hands. He made 166 in England's first innings total of 444 while Australia scored 302 in reply.

England declared on 280 in their second innings, leaving Australia to bat out the allotted time on 371 for nine wickets.

Australian spin bowler Shane Warne claimed his 600th Test wicket during the match. England won the Ashes series 2-1.

Splashing around in the Rochdale Canal!

Here's a rare sight and an absolute treat for children – water levels are so low in the Rochdale Canal at Ancoats that youngsters can paddle in relative safety.

The date is in June 1971 – and part of the canal had been filled in to create a shallow water park. Locks were restored in 1974.

Today's scene, taken from exactly the same angle, tells a different story. Water in the canal is back to its normal level, the saplings of 1971 are now fully grown trees and new buildings have sprung up on left bank.

The Rochdale Canal, runs for 32 miles from the Castlefield Basin in Manchester across the Pennines to Sowerby Bridge in West Yorkshire.

It links the Bridgewater Canal in Manchester with the Calder and Hebble Navigation in Yorkshire.

When it was officially opened in 1804, the Rochdale Canal had 92 locks. After years of restoration, locks three and four were replaced with the Tuel Lane deep lock, reducing the number to 92.

As it was 14ft wide, the Rochdale Canal became more popular than traditional waterways like the Huddersfield Narrow Canal as a route between Lancashire and Yorkshire.

The canal carried 539,081 tons of cargo a year from 1830 to 1832. Major items transported included wool, cotton, coal, limestone, timber and salt.

On July 1st 2002, the Rochdale Canal was once again opened for navigation along its entire length.

Rolling Stones' mania at Belle Vue

Rock band the Rolling Stones perform at a packed New Elizabethan Ballroom at Belle Vue on August 9th 1964.

Visible on stage are guitarist Brian Jones in the foreground with lead singer Mick Jagger just behind him. Guitarist Keith Richards has his back to the camera and drummer Charlie Watts is just out of shot.

Heavy security surrounds the band in the shape of men in suits as over-zealous fans do their best to get a much closer look at their idols!

The Stones were in Manchester as part of their 3rd British tour which included gigs in London, Liverpool and the Channel Islands. They also played Scheveningen in the Netherlands.

Most of June had been spent across the Atlantic as the band had embarked on their first concert tour of the USA to a mixed reception.

Dean Martin was less than kind about their hair and their performance on a TV variety show.

In Chicago, however, the Stones managed to record a cover version of Bobby and Shirley Womack's single It's All Over Now which became their first UK Number One.

Our modern image shows the band 54 years later – again in Manchester. This time they're playing in the open air at Old Trafford in June 2018.

Original group members Jagger, Watts and Richards are still tearing up the stage. On the left is guitarist Ronnie Wood, who joined from the Faces in 1975.

Young Collyhurst cowboy witnesses new era

Bulldozers have reduced terraced homes to rubble in Collyhurst, Manchester, in January 1968 to make way for new high-rise blocks.

The piles of bricks and mortar make a wonderful setting for children's games – especially when you've just got a new cowboy outfit for Christmas!

Slum clearances in Manchester in the 1960s and 1970s were some of the biggest ever witnessed.

Whole streets and communities of terraced houses disappeared.

There truly was optimism – as well as brick dust – in the air.

Major building projects like the Ringway runway extension, the Arndale shopping centre and the M602 motorway all went ahead in the 1970s.

Nowadays, the view from the Sandhills park in Collyhurst is more like a leafy walk than a Wild West frontier.

But blocks of flats can still be glimpsed in our modern image.

Collyhurst quarry provided much of the sandstone used for Manchester buildings, including the cathedral, Chetham's Hospital and St Ann's Church.

Rafts and barges were used to transport stone by river.

It is said that the sandstone for the Roman fort at Castlefield came from Collyhurst.

The area around the disused quarry was turned into the Sandhills park as part of Manchester City Council's Irk Valley Project

Vitamin jabs look painful at the Palace

It looks like an early version of the Covid jab as actresses Jean Muir and Pauline Collins queue up for an injection at the Palace Theatre in August 1965.

The stars were actually getting a vitamin shot to help them cope with all the energetic singing and dancing that went into the musical production Passion Flower Hotel.

The show, based on the novel by Rosalind Erskine, told the light-hearted story of girls at a boarding school getting to know the occupants of a neighbouring boys' school across the lake.

With music by John Barry and lyrics by Trevor Peacock, Passion Flower Hotel premiered in Manchester before moving to the Prince of Wales Theatre in London's West End. It ran for 148 performances.

As well as Collins and Muir, the cast included Francesca Annis, Nicky Henson, Bill Kenwright, Michael Cashman and Jane Birkin. In 1978, Nastassja Kinski starred in a German film loosely based on the story.

Our modern image, from March 2017, shows another musical at the Palace Theatre. This time it's Grease, written by Jim Jacobs and Warren Casey in 1971 and turned into a landmark film starring John Travolta and Olivia Newton-John in 1978.

Lining up at the Palace Theatre are, from left, Darren Day, Louisa Lytton of EastEnders, Danielle Hope and Tom Parker from the band The Wanted.